The Young Scientist Investigates

Small Garden Animals

by
Terry Jennings

CHILDRENS PRESS ®
CHICAGO

Illustrated by
John Barber
Karen Daws

Library of Congress Cataloging-in-Publication Data

Jennings, Terry J.
   Small garden animals.
   (The Young scientist investigates)
   Originally published: Oxford : Oxford University Press, 1981.
   Includes index.
   Summary: Describes invertebrate animals which can be found
in gardens, including insects, spiders, snails, and worms. Includes
review questions and related projects.
   1. Garden fauna—Juvenile literature. [1. Garden animals.]
I. Title. II. Series: Jennings, Terry J. Young scientist investigates.
QL49.J46   1988   592'.05264   88-36216
ISBN 0-516-08442-9

North American edition published in 1989 by
Childrens Press®, Inc.

© Terry Jennings 1982
First published 1982 by Oxford University Press

Printed in the United States of America
1 2 3 4 5 6 7 8 9 10 R 98 97 96 95 94 93 92 91 90 89

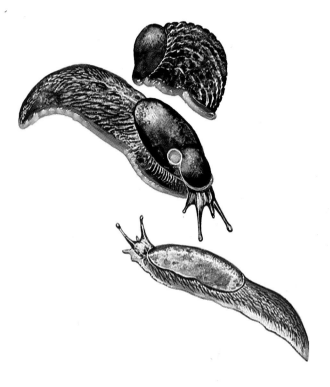

Contents

Animals

There are many different kinds of animals in the world. Some are small like mice and flies. Some are very large, such as elephants and whales.

Scientists divide animals into two groups. Many animals have a backbone inside their bodies. These are called vertebrates. Humans, cows, horses, dogs, cats, mice, frogs, snakes and fishes all have a backbone inside their bodies. They are all vertebrates.

Ants, wasps, flies, bees, snails, wood lice, beetles, spiders and crabs do not have a backbone inside their bodies. They are all invertebrates. Most invertebrate animals are quite small.

Lots of different animals can be found in the garden. A few of them, such as squirrels, mice, moles and rats, are vertebrates. But most of them are invertebrates. This book deals with some of the invertebrate animals that can be found in gardens. If you do not have a garden of your own, you can still find many of them in parks, in the playground or in vacant lots.

Although these animals are common, there is still much we do not know about them. If you study these animals carefully you can learn a lot of new things about them.

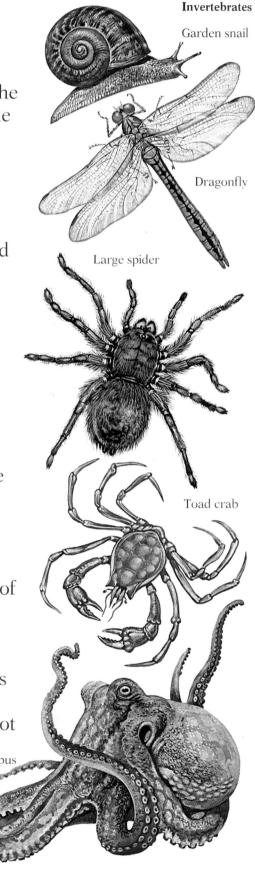

Invertebrates

Garden snail

Dragonfly

Large spider

Toad crab

Common octopus

Crane fly

Vertebrates

Elephant

Pony

Greyhound

Common frog

Grass snake

Field mouse

Flies and other insects

There are many different insects in the garden. Ants, bees, wasps, butterflies, moths, ladybugs, beetles and flies are all insects. Insects do not have backbones. They are invertebrates.

The housefly is a common insect. Like all insects, the housefly's body is in three parts. These parts are the head, the thorax and the abdomen.

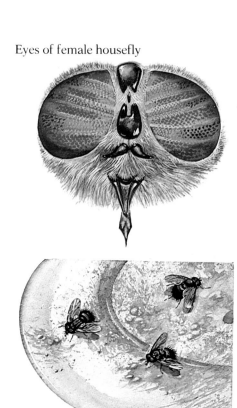

Eyes of female housefly

Housefly

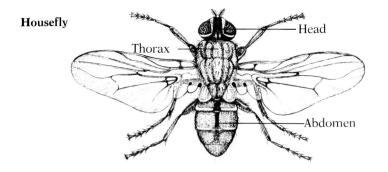

Head

Thorax

Abdomen

The head has a pair of feelers or antennae to feel and to smell with. The head also has two large eyes, each made of thousands of tiny eyes. Eyes like this are called compound eyes.

From the thorax grow the insect's legs and wings. The fly, like all insects, has six legs. It also has two wings.

The housefly is a harmful insect. It feeds on garbage and spreads germs. A housefly lays hundreds of white, oval eggs on garbage and manure. The eggs quickly hatch into larvae or maggots. The maggots feed on the garbage or manure for five days. Then each maggot becomes a hard brown pupa. After four days the pupa splits open and a new housefly crawls out.

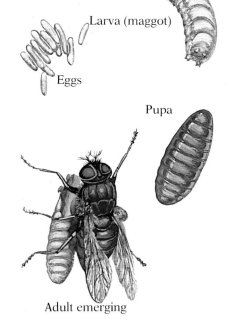

Larva (maggot)

Eggs

Pupa

Adult emerging

4

Ladybugs

Two-spot ladybug

Eyed ladybug

Seven-spot ladybug

Twenty-two spot ladybug

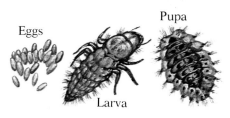

Eggs

Larva

Pupa

Stag beetle

Violet ground beetle

Devil's coach-horse beetle

Furniture beetle

One useful insect is the ladybug. Most ladybugs are red with black spots. But some are yellow with black spots or black with red spots.

Ladybugs are usually found near aphids. Aphids feed on plant juices. They damage many garden plants. Ladybugs eat aphids. They are, therefore, good for the garden.

Ladybugs are a kind of beetle. They have four wings. The front wings are hard and colored. They cover the other two wings, which are thin and delicate. The thin wings are used for flying.

Ladybugs lay their eggs on leaves in summer. The eggs are pale yellow. They hatch into tiny larvae. The ladybug larvae are bluish-black with bright orange spots. The larvae feed on aphids. They may eat 50 aphids in a day.

When the larvae are fully grown, they fix their tails to a leaf. Each larva sheds its skin and becomes a pupa. Eventually a new ladybug crawls out of the pupa.

There are about 300,000 kinds of beetles. Two you often see in gardens are the flea beetle and the Mexican bean beetle. These beetles can cause damage to plants by eating the leaves and spreading plant diseases. But many other beetles help to destroy insect pests.

Butterflies and moths

Peacock

Meadow brown

Small tortoiseshell

Small copper

Small white

Red admiral

Common blue

Peacock butterfly resting (above) and feeding (below)

Caterpillars of peacock butterfly and caterpillar of red admiral butterfly

Butterfly antennae

There are nearly 20,000 kinds of butterflies, but some are very rare. Butterflies fly about in the daytime. You can watch them on sunny days. When it is cloudy or raining, butterflies rest in plants.

All butterflies have four large wings. When butterflies settle, they fold their wings close together. Butterflies have two long antennae. These are very thin and have a small knob on the end.

Garden tiger moth resting

There are more than 100,000 kinds of moths. Most moths fly about at night. During the day they rest in plants. When moths rest, they fold their four wings across their backs. At night moths often fly towards lights. No one knows why they do this.

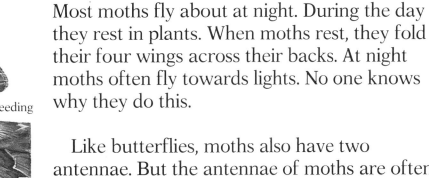

Hawkmoth feeding

Like butterflies, moths also have two antennae. But the antennae of moths are often shaped like a feather or a club. Butterflies and moths cannot eat. Their long tongues are used to sip nectar from flowers.

Butterflies and moths start life as tiny eggs laid on plant leaves. The eggs hatch into small larvae or caterpillars. Caterpillars spend most of their time eating. They eat the leaves on which the eggs are laid. When the caterpillar is fully grown it turns into a pupa or chrysalis. Inside the pupa, the caterpillar gradually changes into the adult butterfly or moth.

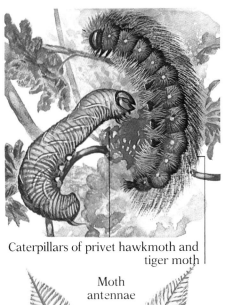

Caterpillars of privet hawkmoth and tiger moth

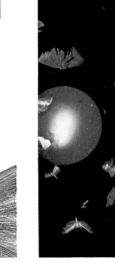

Moth antennae

Moths flying towards a light

The European cabbage butterfly

The European cabbage butterfly is a very common butterfly. It lays its eggs in the early summer. The eggs are laid on the leaves of cabbages, cauliflowers and brussels sprout plants.

After 8 or 10 days the caterpillars hatch out. The caterpillars eat the leaves. As they grow, the caterpillars become too big for their skins. They shed their skins and grow new ones.

After about 30 days the caterpillars stop feeding. Each climbs up a wall, fence or window and spins some silk around itself. The caterpillar's skin splits and it turns into a chrysalis.

In 2 or 3 weeks' time, a rather crumpled butterfly crawls out of the chrysalis. The butterfly spreads its wings to dry. Then it flies off into the sunshine.

European cabbage butterflies also lay eggs in August or September. The caterpillars that hatch from these eggs turn into chrysalises in the autumn. Butterflies are not formed until the spring. Meanwhile the adult butterflies die.

Most butterflies and moths pass the winter in the chrysalis stage. But the red admiral, comma and brimstone butterflies hibernate, or sleep, as adults for the winter. Viceroy butterflies hibernate as caterpillars. Some butterflies fly south for the winter. The European painted lady butterfly flies south to Africa. The American monarch butterfly flies south to Mexico or California for the winter.

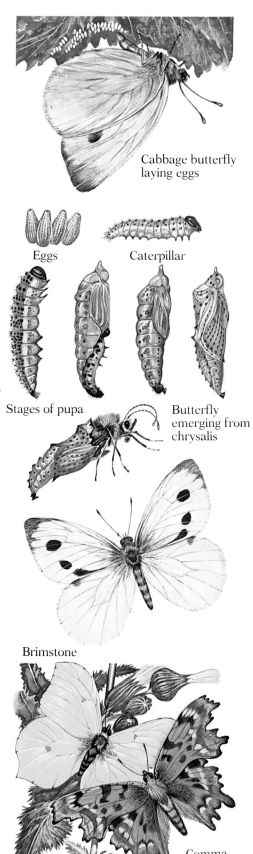

Cabbage butterfly laying eggs

Eggs   Caterpillar

Stages of pupa   Butterfly emerging from chrysalis

Brimstone

Comma

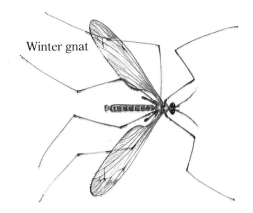
Winter gnat

Gnats and mosquitoes

Everyone has seen swarms of gnats or mosquitoes. They are most often seen in the early evening. These insects have slender bodies and two wings. The male gnat or mosquito feeds on plant juices. It is the female who sucks blood.

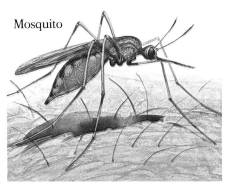
Mosquito

The female gnat or mosquito lands lightly on a person's skin, often when the person is asleep. She pushes her sharp mouthparts into the skin. She forces some of her spit, or saliva, into the blood to stop it clotting. Then she sucks up blood until she is full. The whole meal may take less than 3 seconds. The insect then flies off. The person she bit is left with a small spot that itches.

Mosquito sucking human blood

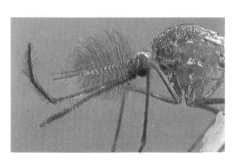

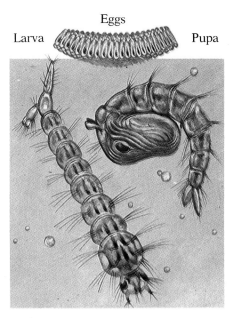
Eggs
Larva   Pupa

Gnats and mosquitoes are never far from water. Their eggs are laid in almost any pool of water, however small. Some gnats and mosquitoes lay their eggs in the water in old tin cans or the stumps of trees.

In a few days a larva breaks out of each egg. Each larva or "wiggler" breathes air through a tube in its abdomen. The larvae grow quickly if the weather is warm. Soon they turn into pupae. The pupae do not feed, although they can move about. After 3 to 5 days the pupae split open and adult gnats or mosquitoes come out.

Honeybees

Queen   Worker   Drone

Wild bees' nest

Some insects live in large groups or colonies and share their work. Ants, bees and many wasps do this.

Many bees are kept in hives. Wild bees and bumblebees make nests in trees or in holes in the ground. There are three kinds of bee in the hive or nest. They are the queen, the workers and the drones.

The queen bee lays the eggs in part of the honeycomb. The drones are the male bees. The drones do not have stingers and they do no work. A drone's only job is to mate with the queen bee.

Bee larvae in cells

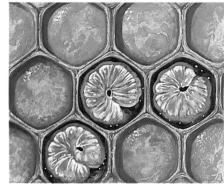

The worker bees are the busiest bees. There are thousands of them in a hive. Worker bees are female and they have stingers. The worker bees make the honeycomb and keep the hive clean. They collect nectar and pollen from flowers. They feed the queen bee and the larvae. Some workers guard the hive and keep it cool by fanning their wings.

Beehive

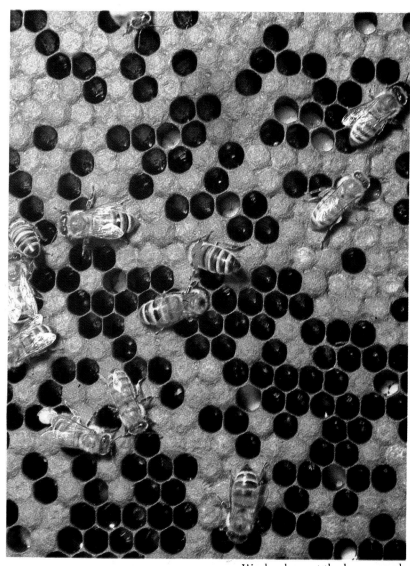

Worker bees at the honeycomb

Honeybees store food so that most of them can live through the winter. They turn the nectar from flowers into honey. The honey is stored in the honeycomb.

Bumblebees do not store honey. So most of the colony dies in the winter. Only the young queen bumblebees live to start a new colony the next year.

Wasps

Some wasps live alone and are called solitary wasps. But most live together in colonies like bees. They are called social wasps.

The queen social wasp builds a nest in the spring. She chooses a hole in the ground, in a tree, the roof of a house or another warm, dry spot. The queen wasp then finds a piece of wood or a tree. She scrapes off pieces of wood, which she chews up until they become a paste. She takes the paste back to her nest site. The paste dries to form a thin sheet of paper. Wasps were the first makers of paper.

At first the paper nest contains just 8 cells. Inside each cell the queen lays an egg. When the eggs hatch, the larvae are fed on insects by the queen. When they are fully grown the larvae turn into pupae.

A few days later, worker wasps leave the cells. The queen lays more and more eggs. The worker wasps now do all the work, including hunting for food, making paper, making the nest bigger and feeding the larvae.

By the end of summer, the nest may be as big as a football and have 25,000 eggs in it. In the autumn the queen stops laying eggs. With nothing to do, the workers look for sweet things like jam and fruit. When the cold weather comes the wasps die. Only a few larvae that turn into queens remain. These leave the nest and find a warm place to sleep for the winter. In the spring each queen builds a new nest.

Solitary wasp (*not to scale*)

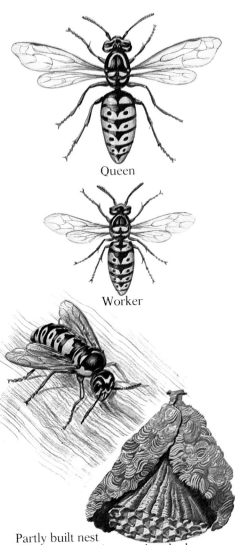

Queen

Worker

Partly built nest
Wasp's nest inside a garden shed

Ants

Wood ants' nest

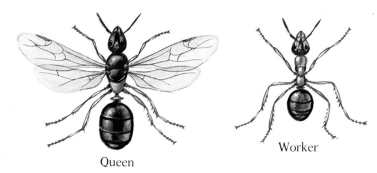

Queen

Worker

Ants always live in colonies. They share the work. Each ant colony has one or two queens whose only job is to lay eggs.

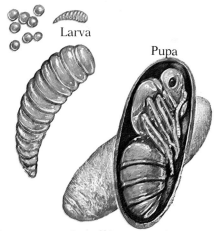

Larva

Pupa

Queen ant tearing off her own wings

Red or black ants are very common in the garden. They live in little tunnels under the soil. Their nest is called an anthill. The queen ant begins to make the nest in the spring. The eggs she lays are very tiny. The eggs hatch into larvae called grubs. The queen feeds these grubs herself. The grubs change into pupae. (The things that many people call ants' eggs and that they feed to fish are really the pupae.)

The young ants that come out are female workers. They have no wings. The workers find food and look after the eggs, grubs and pupae. The workers also make the nest bigger and keep it clean.

Late in the summer, ants are produced that have wings. The larger ones are queens. The smaller winged ants are males. They fly off and mate in the air. When they return to the ground, the males die. The queens break off their own wings. They begin to lay eggs to start new colonies.

Do you remember?

(Look for the answers in the part of the book you have just been reading if you do not know them.)

1 What do scientists call animals that have a backbone inside their bodies?

2 Name six animals that have a backbone inside their bodies.

3 What do scientists call animals that do not have a backbone inside their bodies?

4 Name six animals that do not have a backbone inside their bodies.

5 What are the three parts of an insect's body called?

6 Name six insects.

7 To which part of an insect's body are the wings and legs joined?

8 How many legs do all insects have?

9 How many wings do flies have?

10 What is another name for the feelers of an insect?

11 What is the name given to eyes, such as those of the housefly, that are made of thousands of tiny eyes?

12 What do we often call the larva of a housefly?

13 What colors can ladybugs be?

14 What do ladybugs usually feed on?

15 What are the wings of a ladybug like?

16 What are the wings of a butterfly like, how many of them are there, and where are they kept when the insect is resting?

17 What do caterpillars spend most of their time doing?

18 What is another name for the pupa of a butterfly or moth?

19 When do most moths fly?

20 What are the mouthparts of gnats and mosquitoes like?

21 What do male and female gnats and mosquitoes feed on?

22 What are the three kinds of honeybee?

23 Where is honey stored in a beehive?

24 Name some of the jobs done by worker bees.

25 What do we call the wasps that live alone?

26 What do we call the wasps that live together in colonies like bees?

27 What does the queen wasp do with the little pieces of wood that she scrapes off with her jaws?

28 Where does the queen wasp build her nest?

29 What happens to wasps in winter?

30 What is the main job of queen ants?

Things to do

Small animals are very easily injured. Never pick them up with your fingers or with tweezers. Use a small paintbrush, or a paintbrush and a small spoon. Let the animals go again as soon as possible. Let them go where you found them.

1   Collect pictures of different invertebrates and vertebrates. Write one or two sentences about each one.

2   Make a book or wall chart of pictures of insects. You could draw some of the pictures yourself and collect others from magazines.

3   Keep a record of the insects you see in one particular area. Choose your garden or a small part of a park, the school playground, a backyard or a vacant lot.

Visit the area every day, at the same time if possible. Some time near the middle of the day is best. Keep a note of the insects you see there. Record what the weather is like each day. Say exactly where the insects were and what they were doing. Put the information on a chart like the one below.

In what kinds of weather are most insects to be seen? When do you see the fewest insects? What are the commonest insects in the place where you watched? How many of them are pests? How many are good for the garden?

Date	Time	Weather	Insect	Where seen and what doing
June 30th	11:45 a.m.	Warm and sunny	Ladybug	Resting in the petals of a rose flower
			Ant	Carrying a dead ant to its nest under a stone in the flowerbed

4 Think how you can stop houseflies from spreading disease in your home. Write down as many ways as you can think of.

5 Measure the flight of a ladybug. Carefully put a ladybug on your hand. Blow gently on it. Soon the outer wing-cases will open, the flying wings will unfold and the ladybug will fly away. Follow the ladybug and measure how far it flies.

6 Keep a ladybug in captivity. Use a large jar covered with a piece of cheesecloth or plastic wrap with small holes in it. Keep the ladybug well supplied with pieces of fresh plant on which there are aphids. See how many aphids your ladybug eats in a day. Release the ladybug when you have finished your experiment.

7 Watch the butterflies in the garden. Do they have favorite flowers they visit? Do they have favorite colors of flowers?

8 Try rearing some butterflies or moths. The caterpillar stage is a good starting point. Or you might find some eggs by carefully searching the undersides of leaves. It is important to remember that the caterpillars will only feed on the kind of plant on which you found them (or the eggs).

At first, the eggs or very small caterpillars can be kept in small plastic lunch boxes or small jars. Bigger caterpillars can be housed in large jars or large plastic food containers. If you have two containers, the caterpillars can then be moved to one while the other is being cleaned. Handle the eggs and caterpillars with great care, and do not put more than three or four caterpillars in any one container.

If you do not know whether your caterpillars are those of a butterfly or a moth, put a little soil in the bottom of the container, since many moth caterpillars turn into chrysalises in the soil.

The food plant for the caterpillars can be placed in small pots of damp soil or in little bottles of water plugged with cotton. Do not wait for the food plant to wilt before you put in a fresh one.

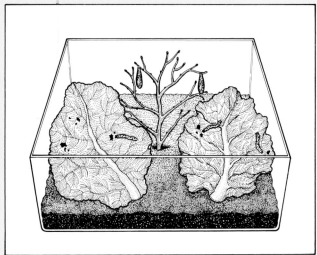

Measure one of the caterpillars every week to see how fast it grows. How often does it molt? How does it get out of its old skin? How many times does it molt before it turns into a chrysalis? If you can, find out how much your caterpillar eats each day.

Release any butterflies or moths that come from the chrysalises in the place where you first found the eggs or caterpillars.

9 Make a clothespin butterfly. Fold a sheet of tracing paper in half. On one half of the tracing paper draw half of a butterfly's head and body and two of its wings. Make sure that the body comes right up to the center fold. Now carefully trace the butterfly onto the other half of the tracing paper. Open out the tracing paper and you have a perfectly shaped butterfly.

Trace your butterfly onto poster board. Cut out the butterfly shape. Paint it in bright colors. Fold up the wings carefully. Paint a clothespin brown. Put a little glue on the underside of the butterfly's body. Glue the butterfly onto the clothespin.

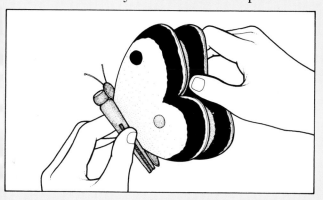

10 Make a collection of cut-out butterflies. Make them the shape, size and color of the common American butterflies.

11 Make a model of a moth. Use modelling clay or papier mâché for the body. Make the wings from thick paper. Use thin wire for the antennae.

12 Think of all the ways in which butterflies and moths are similar and different. Make a list of them.

13 Watch bees visiting flowers in the garden. Make a list of the different kinds of flowers on which they settle. See if they seem to prefer particular colors. Choose one flower and watch it for 30 minutes. How many bees visit the flower during that time? What other insects also visit the flower? Watch carefully to see how the bee collects nectar and pollen. How is the pollen carried away?

14 Make up a play about life in a beehive. Find out what enemies bees have and include them in your play. Make your own costumes and wings. Act your play. Use suitable background music.

15 Have a close look at a dead wasp. Use a magnifying glass or hand lens. Look at the head. Can you see the two large compound eyes? A wasp also has three small eyes on top of its head. Can you see these? Make a large drawing of the wasp.

16 Make a wasps' nest. You can make imitation wasp paper by mixing together water and pieces of torn newspaper to make papier mâché. Make the nest with layers of six-sided cells. Use white modeling clay for the wasp larvae. Make adult wasps out of black and yellow clay. Cut out pieces of cellophane for the wings and use pieces of thin wire for the legs.

17 Imagine ants suddenly grew as big as cats and describe what might happen. Write a story called *The ants attack!*

Garden spiders

The picture shows a garden spider. There are more than 30,000 known kinds of spiders.

All spiders have eight legs. Most have eight simple eyes. Spiders never have wings and their body has only two parts to it. Spiders are not insects. Insects change in some way before they become the adult shape. But little spiders hatch straight from the eggs.

Garden spider

The garden spider makes a beautiful web. The web is built from silken threads made by the spider. The web is used to catch flies or other insects for food. The spider waits in hiding. It runs out if an insect touches the web. The insect is taken to the spider's hiding place to be eaten.

Garden spider wrapping a fly up in silk before she takes it away to eat

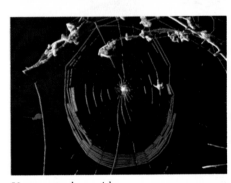
Young garden spiders

In the autumn, the female garden spider hides in a crack and spins a little silk cushion. She lays her eggs on this cushion. Some of the eggs hatch within a few weeks. But many of the eggs stay hidden through the winter.

In the spring young spiders hatch from the eggs. Each young spider spins a silken thread. The wind lifts the young spiders by these threads and blows them over fields, ditches and bushes.

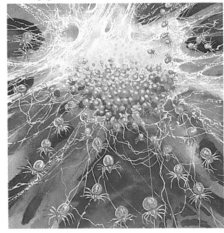

18

House spiders and wolf spiders

House spider

The house spider does not make a beautiful web. Its web is an untidy mass of silk threads. The spider sits in a corner of its web. When an insect is trapped in the web, the spider rushes out and kills it.

You can often find the webs of the house spider in sheds and garages. House spiders also make their webs in the corners of rooms, in cupboards and behind pictures.

Some spiders, such as wolf spiders, do not spin webs at all. They simply run after their food. Wolf spiders move quickly and will attack quite large insects.

The female wolf spider is unusual in that she looks after her eggs and young. She lays eggs in a little fluffy bag or cocoon. The female spider fixes the cocoon to her body with a few strands of silk. She then carries the eggs with her wherever she goes.

When the eggs hatch, the baby spiders run about and feed themselves, but they stay close to their mother. When they are frightened they run to her and climb on her back. If you search among long grass or dead leaves, you will probably see a female wolf spider carrying her eggs or young.

Wolf spider with egg cocoon and wolf spider with young

19

Wood lice

Underneath most old logs, bark, large stones or heaps of dead tree leaves you will find wood lice.

Wood lice are about ½ inch long. Their bodies are covered with hard plates that overlap like the tiles on a roof. A wood louse has seven pairs of legs. It has two eyes and two pairs of feelers or antennae. One pair of antennae is quite large, the other pair is small and hard to see. Wood lice will eat most things but they seem to prefer decaying plant material.

The female wood louse has a little pouch on the underside of her body. In this little pouch she lays her eggs at the beginning of summer. The eggs hatch in the pouch about 5 weeks later. The tiny wood lice run away from their mother's pouch as soon as they are hatched. She takes no more notice of them.

The wood louse's hard outer covering cannot grow. The wood louse has to molt from time to time as it grows bigger. At first the new covering is soft and white, but it quickly hardens and darkens.

One kind of wood louse can roll up in a tight ball when it is frightened. For this reason it is sometimes called a pill bug. Wood lice can live only in damp places. They breathe with gills that must be kept moist. The wood louse is related to the crabs, lobsters, shrimps and barnacles that live in the sea and on the seashore.

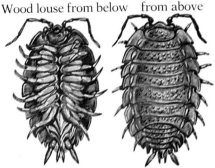

Wood louse from below   from above

Wood louse molting

Pill bug

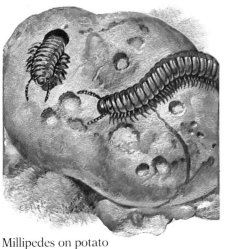

Centipede

Millipede

Centipede

Millipede

Millipedes on potato

Nest and eggs of millipede

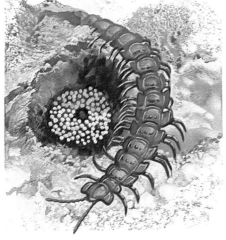

Centipedes and millipedes

Centipedes and millipedes look a little like wood lice. Their bodies are made up of rings or segments. Centipedes and millipedes are usually much longer than wood lice. They also have more than 14 legs.

It is not always easy to tell the difference between a centipede and a millipede. The best way is to look carefully at the segments in the middle of the animal's body. Centipedes have two legs on each segment. Millipedes have four legs on each segment.

Centipedes feed on harmful insects and their larvae. Millipedes eat mainly dead and decaying plants. But sometimes they also eat crop plants.

Millipedes and centipedes live in damp places. You can find them under logs, stones, bark and heaps of dead leaves.

Centipedes lay their eggs in summer. The eggs are sticky and the female rolls each one along the ground. The soil sticks to the eggs so that they look like little lumps of earth. The eggs are then left to hatch.

Some kinds of centipedes lay their eggs in a heap. The young centipedes are guarded by their mother until they can look after themselves. Some millipedes lay their eggs in little nests. Often the female stays with the eggs until they hatch.

21

Snails

Like the wood louse, centipede and millipede, snails also live in dark, damp places. But snails are better protected from enemies than these other animals. A snail has a shell in which it can hide when there is danger.

The shell of a snail is made of a chalky substance. It is made by the snail's body. A snail can pull its whole body into the shell. But it can never leave the shell altogether.

White-lipped snail

Grove snail showing color variation

Garden snail

Door snail

22

The head and tentacles of a snail

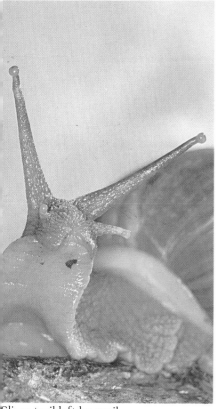

A snail travels along on part of its body called the foot. The snail leaves behind a trail of slime. The slime helps the snail to move along smoothly.

A snail has two pairs of tentacles on its head. The larger pair has eyes on the tips. The smaller pair of tentacles is used for smelling. Snails feed on living and dead plants.

When the weather is very hot or dry, snails stay in their shells. They produce slime that hardens over the entrance to the shell. This seals the shell so that the snail's body does not dry up. In winter snails hibernate in the same way.

Snails lay their eggs in clusters in damp soil. The eggs hatch into tiny snails.

Slime trail left by snail

Snail's eggs hatching

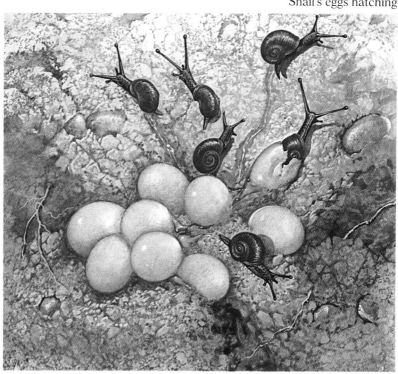

Slugs

Slugs look very much like snails without shells. Some slugs do have a small, oval shell but it is hidden under the skin. Like snails, slugs have a slimy body. They also crawl along over a trail of slime. Slugs also have a pair of tentacles that have eyes and a smaller pair with which they smell things.

Slugs live in moist surroundings. They spend most of the day hidden under logs, stones, or boards or in holes in the ground. The greatest numbers of slugs are to be seen on warm, damp nights.

About a dozen kinds of slugs can be found in gardens. The biggest is the great gray slug, which grows to about 10 inches long. Some kinds are quite small. The hedgehog slug is little more than ½ inch long.

Most slugs will eat almost anything they can find in the garden. Some of their food is the fruit and vegetables we grow for our own use. But much of their food is dead and decaying plant material.

Like snails, slugs are both male and female. But eggs are laid only after two slugs have mated. The eggs are laid in the soil. If the weather is warm and wet, the little slugs hatch about three weeks later. They are able to eat immediately and they grow quickly.

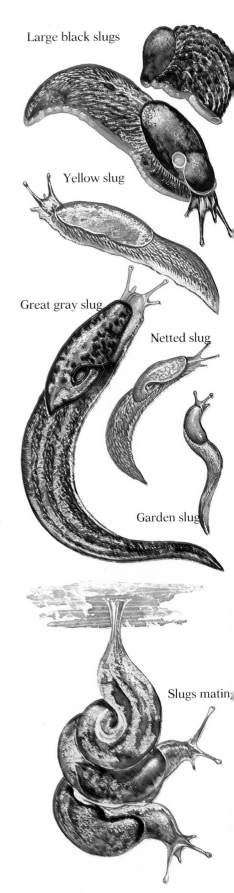

Large black slugs

Yellow slug

Great gray slug

Netted slug

Garden slug

Slugs mating

Great gray slug and eggs

Earthworms

large worm

Earthworms live in burrows in the soil. They stay in their burrows during the day. At night they come to the surface.

Worms have long, soft bodies made up of many rings or segments. They have no eyes, ears or nose but their skin can feel the light. Earthworms can also feel slight movements, or vibrations, of the ground.

Worm casts

Worms eat soil to get the small pieces of decaying plant and animal food they need. The soil passes through their bodies and comes out as worm casts.

Earthworms often pull dead leaves into the soil. There the leaves decay and help to make plants grow better. Earthworms are good for the soil because they mix it up and break it into fine pieces. Their burrows also let air into the soil and help water to drain away.

Like slugs and snails, earthworms are both male and female. But two worms still have to mate before eggs can be laid. Two worms come out of the ground at night and join themselves together with a slimy tube. When they separate, both worms lay eggs. The eggs are laid in a little brown bag, or cocoon, about ¼ inch long. The eggs hatch out into little worms that can look after themselves right away.

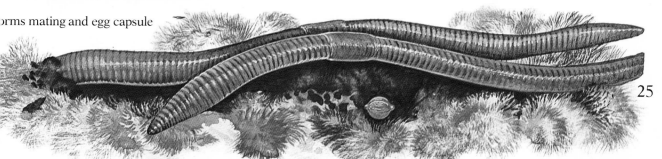

worms mating and egg capsule

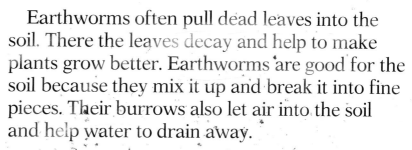

Do you remember?

1 How many legs does a spider have?

2 How many parts are there to a spider's body?

3 What do spiders' eggs hatch into?

4 What is the garden spider's web used for?

5 Where does the garden spider lay her eggs?

6 How do the young garden spiders travel to new places to live?

7 What is the house spider's web like?

8 How does the wolf spider get its food?

9 What does the female wolf spider do with her eggs?

10 What are the bodies of wood lice covered with?

11 How many legs does a wood louse have?

12 Where are the wood louse's eggs laid?

13 Name some of the wood louse's relatives.

14 How can you tell the difference between a centipede and a millipede?

15 What do centipedes and millipedes feed on?

16 When does a snail go into its shell?

17 Why do snails and slugs make a trail of slime?

18 When can you see most slugs?

19 Why are earthworms good for the soil?

20 What are earthworms' eggs laid in?

Things to do

Remember small animals are very easily injured. Never pick them up with your fingers or with tweezers. Use a small paintbrush, or a paintbrush and a small spoon. Let the animals go again as soon as possible. Let them go where you found them.

1 **Make a pitfall trap for small animals.** This type of simple trap can teach you a lot about small animals.

A jam jar, a smooth-sided can or a yogurt cup is needed. Bury the container on a lawn, in a flower bed, under a hedge, on a vacant lot or somewhere else where you think small animals might be. Bury the container so that the top is level with the surface of the ground. Bait the trap with pieces of bread, vegetables, scraps of meat, dog food, and so on.

Put two stones or pieces of wood at opposite sides of the top of the trap. Lay a piece of wood or a tile over the top to keep out the rain. Leave the trap for several hours, or overnight if you want to catch some of the small animals that come out at night.

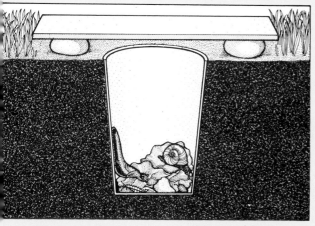

Keep records of what kinds of animals you are able to trap in different parts of the garden and with different baits. Do the numbers and kinds of animals you catch differ according to the weather or the time of the year?

It is important that you dig up these traps when you have finished with them, or cover them over so that animals cannot get in them. If you forget the traps or leave them, large numbers of small animals may die.

2   Try another way of catching small animals. Lay pieces of wood or black plastic on the ground in the garden or school grounds. Leave the wood or plastic undisturbed for a few days. Then have a look at what you find underneath it. The wood or plastic will make grass turn yellow for a few days, so make sure you

have permission if you put it on the lawn.

You might also like to put pieces of bait down and then cover these with wood or black plastic. Try different baits like dog food, jam, honey, sugar, bread, a piece of apple or tomato, and so on. Leave the bait for several hours or overnight. Then see what has come to it.

If you have a strong net, you can sweep it through long grass or beds of stinging nettles and other weeds. Look in the net from time to time to see what you have caught.

On hot, sunny days, it is fun to see what effect artificial rain has on small animals in the garden. Water the grass thoroughly with a fine spray from a sprinkler. What animals appear?

3   Search your garden for small animals. Record the kinds of animals you find and where you find them.

Look in the cracks in the bark of a tree and on the undersides of leaves. Look for the animals that live in decaying wood. Turn over any rotting logs, stones, bricks, or planks of wood lying on the ground, but afterwards put these things back exactly as they were; otherwise, the animals will die.

Lay a sheet of cloth or plastic under a tree. Knock the branch above it with a stick. See what has fallen onto the sheet.

Place a large cloth or plastic bag over a low branch of a tree. Shake the branch firmly, being careful not to damage the tree. Look at any animals that have fallen into the bag.

Try to name all the animals you find. You might draw a table like this one:

Date	Place	Name of animal	Number of animals
July 30th	Trunk of oak tree in garden	Ant	7
	Under old brick	Slug	2

Let the animals go again as soon as possible after you have looked at them. Put them in the exact place where you found them.

4   Look for spiders to keep in captivity. Search for them in dark corners, under rocks, stones and logs, and in cracks in fence posts and bark.

Almost any container can be used to house spiders. Jam jars, candy jars, plastic food containers or large cans are all suitable. Use a piece of net curtain, or plastic wrap with holes in it, for the top. Put only one spider in the container.

Some spiders like a dark place to hide in, so an open matchbox should be placed in one corner. A branching twig will support any webs the spider makes. Put a few stones, leaves and pieces of damp moss in the container as well.

The house spider also thrives in captivity. A large jar in which a roll of paper is placed will make a good home for one of these spiders.

The food for the spiders must be *live* flies and other small invertebrates. Water is also necessary, which is why you will often find a spider in the bathtub. Put some water in a small dish or bottle top, or in a little bottle with a loose plug of cotton, which will then be kept moist.

Try to watch the spiders building their webs. See how they catch their food. How much do they eat? What parts of an insect do they not eat? When are the spiders most active?

5   Find out whether spiders mend their webs. Very gently cut part of a web. The next day, see whether or not it has been mended.

6   Find out how long a spider keeps its web. Mark webs by placing tiny pieces of tissue paper on the sticky threads. Check each morning and evening to see how long the webs remain.

7   Write a story. Imagine you could become as small as a fly. You fall into a spider's web. Tell the story of how you escape being eaten. You could draw some pictures to illustrate the tale.

8   Keep some wood lice in captivity. They are easy to keep. A large jar is an ideal container. The air in the container must always be damp. A layer of moist soil in the bottom of the jar with plenty of moss over the top will keep the air damp. It is a good idea to put a small lump or two of chalk in the container to help the wood lice make their hard outer covering.

Keep the wood lice in a shady place. Give them plenty of pieces of plant material for food, and particularly pieces of potato peelings. Clean the container out about every two or three weeks. The wood lice will soon settle down to breed.

9   Keep some snails and slugs. They can be kept in a variety of containers. There should be air holes in the top of the container, but the air must always be damp if the animals are to be active.

The bottom of the container should have a layer of at least 3 inches of moist soil and, if there is room, small clumps of grass.

Put no more than two or three large

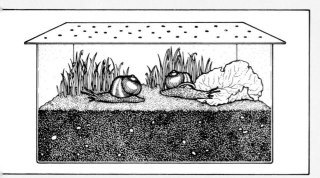

slugs or snails in a container. Up to six or eight of the smaller kinds will live in each container.

Feed the snails with a smear of flour paste, mashed potato, or cabbage or lettuce leaves. Slugs prefer fresh cabbage and lettuce leaves and also pieces of carrot. When vegetables are scarce, almost any weed leaves, particularly those of stinging nettles, will do for both slugs and snails. Get rid of the stale food each day and put in fresh food. Clean out the container every two or three weeks.

After a time, look for eggs below the surface of the soil. Carefully move the eggs to jam jars or flower pots of moist soil. Cover the jars or pots with plastic wrap in which tiny air holes have been punched.

10   Have a close look at a slug or a snail. Let the animal crawl up the inside of a clean jar. Look at it from the other side. What do you see? How does the animal move? Where does the slime come from?

Let the slug or snail crawl across a sheet of damp paper. Put an obstacle such as a piece of wood in its way. How does the animal get past it?

Gently touch the slug or snail's back with a pencil. What does it do?

Can you see the slug or snail's mouth? How does it eat? If you listen quietly can you hear it eating? Look at the slug or snail's eyes with a hand lens or magnifying glass. Can you see the animal's breathing hole? It is on the right-hand side of the body. When does this hole open? Does it ever close completely?

11   Compare the speeds of different kinds of slugs and snails. Draw a circle 24 inches across on a sheet of paper. Make a small circle the size of a dime coin in the center of the bigger circle.

Put a slug or snail in the small circle and time how long it takes to travel the 12 inches to the outside of the big circle. Compare the speeds of slugs and snails with those of centipedes, millipedes and other small invertebrates.

Experiments to try

Do your experiments carefully. Write or draw what you have done and what happens. Say what you have learned. Compare your findings with those of your friends.

1 How quickly do aphids breed?

Most of the time aphids do not lay eggs. Each one can produce small living young. Do this experiment in the summer.

What you need: A leafy twig from a rose bush; a small paintbrush; one fat aphid; a jar with a lid.

What you do: Carefully wash the twig of the rose bush to make sure there are no aphids on it. Shake the water off the twig and then put it into the jar. With the paint-brush, gently lift the aphid onto one of the leaves of the rose twig. Punch some holes in the lid and put the lid on the jar.

Look at the twig after one day, and then again after two days, and so on. How many aphids are there each day?

If you can, do this experiment again with more aphids, rose twigs and jars. Put one aphid on a twig in a jar that you keep in a cold place, another in a warm place, and another in the dark. What happens? Do the aphids breed as quickly in each of the jars?

2 Ants and food

What you need: Four or five small jar tops; some little pieces of meat, cookies and bread; a spoonful of sugar, jam, marmalade or any other sweet foods. You also need to find an ants' nest in the garden.

What you do: Put a tiny piece of meat or cooky near the ants' nest. See how many ants come to the food. Do they pull the food to the nest? Now put down another piece of food twice as big as the first. Do twice as many ants arrive to pull it into the nest?

Next put down four or five small jar tops in a row near the ants' nest. Put a little jam in one, a little sugar in another, a little marmalade in another, a few cooky or bread crumbs in the next, and so on. Which top do the ants go to first? Which top do the most ants go to? Do they take any of the foods to the nest? Now try the experiment with other kinds of foods.

3 What conditions do wood lice like best?

What you need: Two small clear glass jars, both the same size; some clear tape; some black paper or cloth; paper towels; coffee filter paper or cotton; ice cubes; some wood lice.

What you do: Lay the two jars on their sides. Put 5 or 6 wood lice just inside one of the jars, and then tape the necks of the jars together. Quickly cover one jar with black paper or cloth, so that one jar is now dark inside while the other is light. Leave the jars for 10 minutes. Then see how many wood lice there are in each jar. Do this several times.

Do the wood lice like the light or the dark jar best? Does it matter which jar you put the wood lice in first?

Now start again with the two jars. Put a dry piece of paper towel, filter paper or wool in one jar, a wet piece of the same material in the other. Put in the wood lice, and tape the jars together. Do not cover either jar with black cloth or paper this time. Leave the jars for 10 minutes. Then see how many wood lice there are in each jar. Do this several times. Do the wood lice like the dry jar or the damp jar best?

Repeat the experiment, but this time pack ice cubes around the outside of one jar. Leave the other jar as it is. Do the wood lice prefer the cold jar or the warmer one?

Do this experiment with other animals. Snails, slugs, centipedes, millipedes and maggots are good ones to try. So far we have given the animals choices between light and dark, damp and dry, warm and cold. Can you think of any other choices you could give them in an experiment like this?

4 Which foods do slugs like best?

What you need: A large plastic sandwich box; some paper towels or coffee filter paper; some plant leaves of different kinds; some slugs.

What you do: Wet a paper towel or some filter paper and lay it on the bottom of the sandwich box. Take one leaf of each kind. Arrange the leaves in a circle around the bottom of the box.

Into the middle of the circle put 4 or 5 large slugs or 10 small ones, all of the same kind. Cover the box with a sheet of plastic wrap in which there are small air holes.

Leave the box for two days. Then see which leaves have been eaten. How much of each leaf has been eaten? You should now know which kinds of leaves slugs like the best and which kinds they like the least.

Try this experiment with tree leaves, vegetable leaves, the leaves of flowering plants, and with different kinds of slugs. You could also try this experiment with snails, millipedes and wood lice.

5 Do snails return to the same place?

What you need: A small paintbrush; some quick-drying paint.

What you do: Find some snails in the garden. Mark their shells with little dabs of paint. If the snails are large ones, you can paint numbers on their shells. Make a note of where you found each snail.

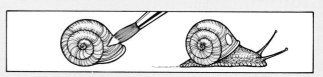

Visit the place where the snails were marked each night and morning for several days. If you cannot find the snails, try to follow their slime trails to see where they have gone.

Can you find out how far the snails travel each night? Where do they go to? What do they feed on? Do they return to the same place each time? How long do they stay there?

Glossary

Here are the meanings of some words that you might have met for the first time in this book.

Abdomen: the back part of the body of an insect or a spider. The part of a human containing the stomach.

Antenna: one of the feelers on an insect, wood louse or other invertebrate animal.

Caterpillar: the larva of a butterfly or moth.

Chrysalis: the pupa or resting stage of a butterfly or moth, in which the adult insect develops.

Cocoon: a silky case in which eggs are laid or in which a pupa is formed.

Compound eye: an eye, such as that of the housefly, that consists of thousands of simple eyes.

Hibernate: to sleep for the winter.

Invertebrate: an animal that does not have a backbone inside its body. Most invertebrate animals are quite small.

Larva: the stage in the life of an insect that comes from the egg. Maggots, caterpillars and grubs are examples of larvae.

Maggot: another name for the larva of a fly.

Pupa: the resting stage in the life of an insect in which the adult insect develops.

Saliva: the spit or liquid formed inside the mouth of an animal.

Social: a word used to describe an animal or person who likes the company of others of the same kind.

Solitary: a word used to describe an animal or person who likes to be alone.

Tentacle: a long, slender feeler on the head of a slug or snail. Some tentacles carry the animal's eyes.

Thorax: the part of an animal's body between the head and abdomen. The thorax of an insect has the legs and wings growing from it.

Vertebrate: an animal that has a backbone inside its body.

Vibration: a very slight movement.

Acknowledgments

The publishers would like to thank the following for permission to reproduce transparencies:

Heather Angel: p. 5 and back cover; Ardea London/ A. Warren: p. 7; Bruce Coleman Ltd: S. C. Bisserot p. 13, J. Burton p. 18 (left), R. Longo p. 11 (right) and front cover, J. Markham p. 12, L. L. Rue p. 10, K. Taylor p. 9 (right) and S. Trevor p. 23; Oxford Scientific Films: p. 9 (left), p. 11 (left) and p. 18.

Index